TIMELINE OF MARY CASSATT'S LIFE

 1844 Mary Cassatt is born in Allegheny City, Pennsylvania.

 1851 Mary's parents move the family to Europe. There she sees paintings by some of the world's greatest artists.

 1855 Mary and her family return to Pennsylvania.

 1860 Mary Cassatt decides she wants to be an artist and enters the Academy of Fine Arts in Philadelphia.

 1865 Mary moves to Paris, France, the art center of the world at the time. She becomes the student of Jean-Léon Gérôme, a well-known painter.

 1868 Mary's painting *A Mandolin Player* is accepted by the Paris Salon.

 1870 When war breaks out between France and Germany, Mary returns to the United States. However, she returns to Paris the next year.

THIS WAY

UP HERE

 **1872** Mary travels to Parma, Italy, to study great Italian artists. The next year, she visits Spain, Belgium, and the Netherlands before making Paris her permanent home.

 1877 Mary's artist friend Edgar Degas invites her to join the Impressionist artists. The next year Mary begins working closely with Degas.

 1886 Two of Mary's paintings are displayed at the first Impressionist exhibition in the United States.

 1891 Mary begins a huge mural for the 1893 Columbian Exposition in Chicago.

 1894 Mary Cassatt buys a large house outside of Paris.

 1914 Mary begins to lose her eyesight and has to give up painting. She continues to exhibit her work, and keeps busy at her chateau.

 1926 Mary Cassatt dies at her home, Chateau de Beaufresne.

GETTING TO KNOW THE WORLD'S GREATEST ARTISTS

MARY CASSATT

WRITTEN AND ILLUSTRATED BY MIKE VENEZIA

CONSULTANT SARA MOLLMAN UNDERHILL

CHILDREN'S PRESS®

An Imprint of Scholastic Inc.

New York   Toronto   London   Auckland   Sydney
Mexico City   New Delhi   Hong Kong
Danbury, Connecticut

For the special girls in my life,
Elizabeth, Laura, and Brigette

Cover: *The Child's Bath.* 1893, oil on canvas,
100.3 x 66.1 cm (39 1/2 x 26 in.). Robert A. Waller Fund,
1910.2, The Art Institute of Chicago

Library of Congress Cataloging-in-Publication Data
Venezia, Mike, author, illustrator.
  Mary Cassatt / written and illustrated by Mike Venezia.
  – Revised edition.
     pages cm. – (Getting to know the world's greatest artists)
  Summary: "Introduces the reader to the artist Mary Cassatt"–
Provided by publisher.
  Audience: 8-9.
  Includes bibliographical references and index.
  ISBN 978-0-531-21315-5 (library binding : alk. paper)
– ISBN 978-0-531-21292-9 (pbk. : alk. paper)
  1. Cassatt, Mary, 1844-1926–Juvenile literature. 2. Painters–United
States–Biography–Juvenile literature. 3. Women painters–United
States–Biography–Juvenile literature. I. Title. II. Series: Venezia, Mike.
Getting to know the world's greatest artists.

  ND237.C3V46 2015
  759.13–dc23
  [B]

2014042742

1 2 3 4 5 6 7 8 9 10 R 24 23 22 21 20 19 18 17 16 15

Self-portrait. c. 1880.
Watercolor on paper,
13 x 9⅝ inches.
National Portrait Gallery,
Smithsonian Institution

Mary Cassatt was born in Allegheny, Pennsylvania, in 1844. She is known as a great American artist, even though she spent most of her life living and painting in France.

After the Bath. 1901. Pastel, 25¾ x 39¼ inches.
The Cleveland Museum of Art. Gift from J.H. Wade

Mary Cassatt loved families and
children. Her paintings and pastels of
mothers with their babies are among
her most famous works.

Mother About to Wash Her Sleepy Child. 1880. Oil on canvas, 39½ x 25¾ inches.
Los Angeles County Museum of Art. Mrs. Fred Hathaway Bixby Bequest

When Mary was seven years old,
her family left America and moved to
Paris, France, for a couple of years.
Mr. and Mrs. Cassatt wanted their

children to see all the wonderful
sights while they lived in Paris. They
took their children to the great art
museums and galleries, where Mary
saw her first works of art.

A few years after the Cassatt family returned to America, Mary decided she wanted to be an artist. Not just any artist, but a serious artist. At first, Mary's father was very upset.

In the 1880s, people felt women weren't supposed to be artists. They thought women should only have very polite hobbies, become someone's wife, and stay home to raise their children.

It was one of the few times Mary and her father didn't get along.

Finally, after realizing how much Mary wanted to be an artist, her father agreed to send her to art school.

Mary studied very hard at the Pennsylvania Academy of the Fine Arts. After four years there, she decided a better way to learn about art would be to copy the paintings of the world's great artists.

There were very few paintings by
great artists in America at that time,
so in 1865 Mary Cassatt left for
France. She spent as much time as
she could in art museums, copying
famous paintings.

Mary Cassatt was becoming a pretty good artist. So she entered one of her paintings in the Paris Salon.

The Salon was an important place to have your paintings shown. People from all over the world came to look at—and maybe buy—the paintings they saw there.

It wasn't easy getting a painting into the Paris Salon. It was even harder if you were a woman artist, especially an *American* woman artist.

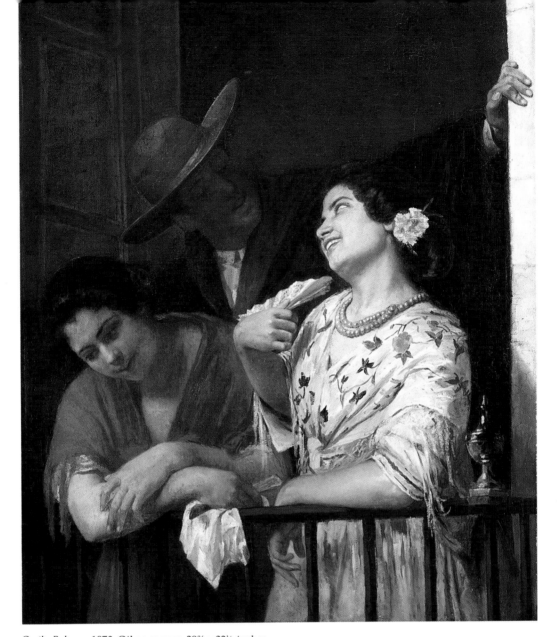

On the Balcony. 1873. Oil on canvas, 39¾ x 32½ inches.
Philadelphia Museum of Art. The W.P. Wilstach Collection

But in 1872, Mary's painting *On the Balcony* was accepted by the judges of the great Salon.

The Salon accepted four more of Mary Cassatt's paintings. Then something happened that changed Mary's life.

At that time, a small group of artists called Impressionists were painting in new and exciting ways.

They didn't like the rules the Salon had made about the way art should look. They didn't think the Salon's judges should decide what was good or bad about paintings either.

One of the Impressionists, Edgar Degas, asked Mary to join their group.

Mary was thrilled.

Mary had seen
paintings done by
the Impressionists.
She loved the bright,
beautiful colors
that Claude Monet,
Camille Pissarro, Auguste
Renoir, and the other
Impressionists used.

The Artist's Garden at Vetheuil.
1880. By Claude Monet,
oil on canvas, 59⅝ x 47⅝ inches.
National Gallery of Art, Washington.
Ailsa Mellon Bruce Collection

Boulevard des Italiens, Morning, Sunlight. 1897.
By Camille Pissarro,
oil on canvas, 28⅞ x 36¼ inches.
National Gallery of Art, Washington.
Chester Dale Collection

Right: *A Girl with a Watering Can.* 1876.
By Auguste Renoir,
oil on canvas, 38½ x 28¾ inches.
National Gallery of Art, Washington.
Chester Dale Collection

16

The Dancers. c. 1899. By Edgar Degas. Pastel on paper, 24½ x 25½ inches.
The Toledo Museum of Art, Toledo, Ohio. Gift of Edward Drummond Libbey

But, most of all, Mary liked the
work of Edgar Degas. She thought his
colors, unusual angles, and the way
he painted people made his paintings
perfect.

Mary Cassatt and Edgar Degas became close friends. Mary learned all she could from Degas. Soon she stopped using dark background colors and painting people in fancy costumes like in the painting above. She stopped doing things the judges at the Salon would have accepted.

Little Girl in a Blue Armchair. 1878. Oil on canvas, 35¼ x 51⅛ inches.
National Gallery of Art, Washington. Collection of Mr. and Mrs. Paul Mellon

She started to paint people as they
really looked, doing everyday things.
Her colors got brighter, too.

In the Omnibus (The Tramway). 1891. Drypoint, soft-ground and aquatint printed in color on three plates. Mr. and Mrs. Martin A. Ryerson Collection. Photograph © 1990, The Art Institute of Chicago.

Mary kept working with Edgar Degas. They experimented with different types of art. For a while, Mary made a series of special color prints.

Women Admiring a Child. 1897. Pastel, 26 x 32 inches. © The Detroit Institute of Arts.
Gift of Edward Chandler Walker

They also experimented with pastels, mixing them with oil, turpentine, and even steam. They were trying to find ways to make the chalky colors as bright as possible and make the pastels sink deep into the paper.

In 1877, Mary's mother, father, and sister, Lydia, came to live with her in Paris. Her brothers and their families would visit Mary, too. Mary used the members of her family as models in many of her paintings and pastels.

Woman and Child Driving. 1881. Oil on canvas, 35¼ x 51½ inches.
Philadelphia Museum of Art. The W.P. Wilstach Collection

In the painting above, Mary
showed her sister, Lydia, driving a
carriage. Mary was interested in
photography and framed this
painting so the pony and carriage are
cut off. Mary knew that framing her
painting like a snapshot would give
more importance to her sister and the
little girl sitting next to her.

In 1892, Mary was very happy to receive an invitation from America. She was asked to make a huge painting, called a mural, for the Woman's Building at the Chicago World's Fair. The painting was so large that the canvas had to be lowered into a ditch while Mary was working on it so that she could reach the top!

Baby Reaching for an Apple.
1893. Oil on canvas,
39½ x 25¾ inches.
Virginia Museum of
Fine Arts, Richmond

The painting mysteriously
disappeared after the fair. Some
people think the smaller painting
shown above may have been a study
for Mary's huge painting.

Breakfast in Bed. 1897. Oil on canvas, 25⅝ x 29 inches. Henry E. Huntington Library and Art Gallery, San Marino, California. The Virginia Steele Scott Collection

Mary Cassatt never had children of her own, but she seemed to understand the love between mothers and their babies better than any other artist.

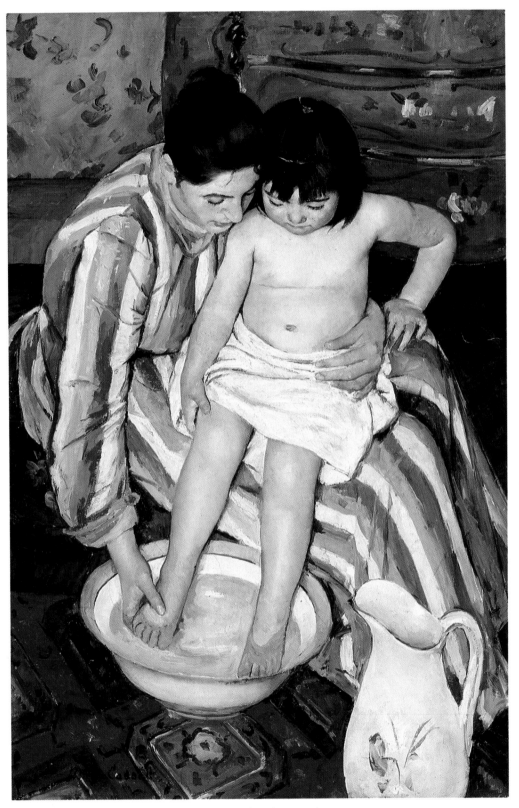

The Child's Bath. 1893, oil on canvas, 100.3 x 66.1 cm (39 1/2 x 26 in.).
Robert A. Waller Fund, 1910.2., The Art Institute of Chicago

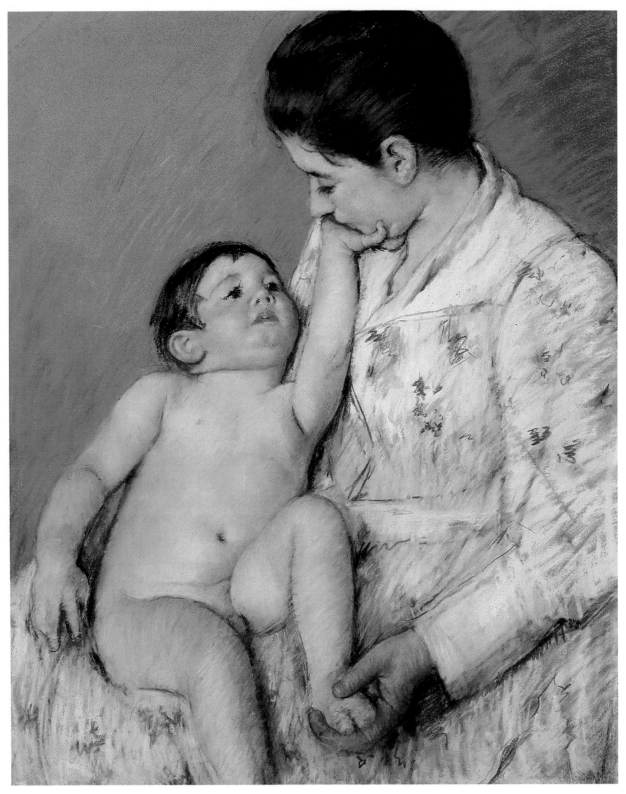

Baby's First Caress. 1891. Pastel, 30 x 24 inches. From the collection of the New
Britain Museum of American Art, Connecticut. Harriet Russell Stanley Fund

The Boating Party. 1893-1894. Oil on canvas, 35½ x 46⅛ inches.
National Gallery of Art, Washington. Chester Dale Collection

Whether she used soft pastels or strong shapes and bright colors, Mary Cassatt's pictures are always warm and friendly.

Mary Cassatt's paintings make you feel like you're right there, looking in on someone during a special moment.

Mother and Child. c. 1890. Oil on canvas, 35⅜ x 25⅜ inches. Courtesy Wichita Art Museum, Wichita, Kansas. The Roland P. Murdock Collection

She made ordinary, everyday scenes important,

Girl Arranging Her Hair. 1886. Oil on canvas, 29½ x 24½ inches. National Gallery of Art, Washington. Chester Dale Collection

and helped make
the world realize
that women could
be great artists, too.

At the Theatre. 1879.
Pastel on paper, 21¹³⁄₁₆ x 18⅛ inches.
The Nelson-Atkins Museum of Art,
Kansas City, Missouri. Anonymous gift

Mary Cassatt
painted with love,
in a way few
artists have ever
been able to do.

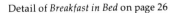
Detail of *Breakfast in Bed* on page 26

It's fun to see real Mary Cassatt paintings. When you look closely, you'll be surprised at how she used little flecks of color to make eyes and noses, and to capture the delicate expressions on her people's faces.

The pictures in this book came from the museums listed below:

The Art Institute of Chicago, Chicago, Illinois
The Cleveland Museum of Art, Cleveland, Ohio
The Detroit Institute of Art, Detroit, Michigan
Henry E. Huntington Library and Art Gallery, San Marino, California
Los Angeles County Museum of Art, Los Angeles, California
Montclair Art Museum, Montclair, New Jersey
National Gallery of Art, Washington, D.C.
National Portrait Gallery, Washington, D.C.
The Nelson-Atkins Museum of Art, Kansas City, Missouri
New Britain Museum of American Art, New Britain, Connecticut
Philadelphia Museum of Art, Philadelphia, Pennsylvania
The Toledo Museum of Art, Toledo, Ohio
Virginia Museum of Fine Arts, Richmond, Virginia
Wichita Art Museum, Wichita, Kansas

LEARN MORE BY TAKING THE CASSATT QUIZ!

(ANSWERS ON THE NEXT PAGE.)

1. Mary Cassatt loved dogs. Her pets can be seen in many of her paintings. What was Mary's favorite breed of dog?
- a Brussels griffons
- b Brussels sprouts
- c Australian dingos

2. Besides being an artist, what else was Mary Cassatt known for?
- a Guiding people on fishing expeditions through France
- b Helping wealthy Americans choose great works of art for their collections
- c Conducting French cooking classes

3. Mary wasn't the only woman to join the Impressionist group. Who was another famous woman Impressionist artist?
- a Berthe Morisot
- b Judy Collins
- c Rachel Carson

4. Why did Mary's father object so much when she announced she wanted to leave home, travel to Paris, and start a career as an artist?
- a He wanted her to stay at home until she cleaned up her room.
- b He thought women should take up painting only as a hobby, not as a serious career.
- c He wanted to keep his children close to him.

5. Mary was very generous helping young American art students. Before giving them financial assistance, though, she sometimes asked them to:
- a Mow her lawn for one year
- b Study the works of master artists in European museums
- c Walk her dogs whenever it rained

ANSWERS

1. **a** Mary loved little dogs. Her favorite breed was the Brussels griffon. You can see one of Mary's pet griffons on page 19 of this book.

2. **b** Mary Cassatt was known for advising her wealthy American art collector friends. Mary helped them choose works by Impressionist artists as well as European masters of the past. Most of Mary's friends eventually donated their paintings to America's art museums. Many of the best works of art in the world are in the United States, thanks to Mary's good advice.

3. **a** Along with Mary Cassatt, Berthe Morisot was one of three well-known women Impressionist artists. The other was Marie Bracquemond. All three were important contributors to the Impressionist art movement.

4. **b and c** In the late 1800s, it wasn't considered acceptable for women from wealthy families to have a career. Mary's father believed it was his job to take care of the women in his family. Robert Cassatt was also very close to his family and wanted to keep everyone nearby.

5. **b** Mary not only donated money for student scholarships, but she spent time giving advice to American students. Sometimes Mary required that the money she offered be used to study and copy art works in European museums.